let the children come to me

SHERON BURTON

let the children come to me

Bible Stories for Children

WESTBOW
PRESS®
A DIVISION OF THOMAS NELSON
& ZONDERVAN

WestBow Press books may be ordered through booksellers or by contacting:

WestBow Press
A Division of Thomas Nelson & Zondervan
1663 Liberty Drive
Bloomington, IN 47403
www.westbowpress.com
844-714-3454

ISBN: 978-1-6642-0841-4 (sc)
ISBN: 978-1-6642-0970-1 (e)

Print information available on the last page.

WestBow Press rev. date: 10/27/2020

Thank you for accurate accounts of Bible stories that can be read to our children that speak the truth and not a television version made for a movie. I expected nothing less from you. May God Bless!

— Claudette Arnold Youth Pastor

dedication

This work is dedicated to a Bible study youth group, S.A.L.T. (SAVE A LIFE TODAY) that I taught several years ago. They informed me during a Bible study that they would like to read the Bible more but did not understand the Bible, and that inspired me to write this work.

acknowledgments

I would like to acknowledge my husband, Minister Alfred Charles Burton; he is the consummate advocate and supporter in whatever the Lord endeavors for me to do, and I love him for being a humble man of God.

To my daughter, Clarissa Louise Johnson, who attended the youth Bible study group (S.A.L.T.) that I taught. She was one of the youths that spoke a truth that inspired this work; "Out the mouths of babes and nursing infants.You have perfected praise." (Matthew 21:16 NKJV).

To two of Gods' angels and my spiritual parents, Pastor and Sister Calvin Arnold, who have always believed in me and encouraged me to be the best me I can be for the Lord.

table of contents

foreword

Welcome to Sharon Burton's impressive work titled *Let the Children Come to Me: Bible Stories for Children*. In this concise, point-by-point book, you will experience a unique vision in reaching young people with Biblical stories. A conversational format causes the reader to see a present-day relationship with the message.

Sharon has been given a visionary gift for ministering to today's youth. From Adam's tragedy to the Savior's triumph, each chapter's inquiry compels you toward a personal acknowledgement of the d ivine truth. Sharon has blessed us with a book that teaches a new generation of kingdom workers.

Calvin Arnold
Pastor, The Church at Caldwell Ministries
Caldwell, Texas

introduction

Many, many, many years ago "they brought little children to Him, that He might touch them; but the disciples rebuked those who brought them." (Mark 10:13 NKJV).

When Jesus saw this, he was angry. He said to them, "Let the little children come to Me, and do not forbid them, for of such is the kingdom of God." (Mark 10:14 NKJV).

Please do not be misled by the title of this work, *Let the Children Come to Me: Bible Stories for Children,* for the Bible tells us that we are all God's children and all of God's children are special to him.

Oftentimes children hear Bible stories through the voice of adults. Children in the Bible had a perspective of their own. All of God's children need to hear Bible stories in their voice to understand what God expects of them.

These compelling stories will speak volumes to adults as well and help them remember their own childhood. The Bible tells us no one can see the kingdom of God unless he is born again (John 3:5 NKJV). For the Bible tells us God called us all to be born-again and to be newborns, spiritually.

It is very important to understand children in the Bible and the children in our lives because they are the nation God is raising up to a new dimension of faith.

adam and eve's home in the garden

Years and years and years ago there was only one person in the whole world. He had only one name and a very short name at that—it was Adam! This was a very long time ago, before there were any automobiles, trains, telephones, radios, and television sets. It was so long ago that no houses had been built. In fact, there was no one to build houses, and no one to live in them if they had been built. Adam did not even have a bed on which to sleep! Perhaps you would like to know how long ago it was that Adam lived all alone? It was many, many, many years ago. That is a long time, isn't it?

Adam had no house, but we must not think he didn't have a nice place in which to live. After God made Adam, he planted a beautiful, big garden that he called Eden. There were so many wonderful flowers and trees in that garden. They were the most beautiful flowers and trees that anybody has ever seen. There were plenty of nice vegetables, and every fruit you can think of.

And God put Adam into this perfect garden to take care of it, and to enjoy it forever. Wouldn't you like to live in a place like that, forever and ever? While there were no men, women, or children to keep Adam company, he was not all alone because the Bible tells us that there were many birds and animals in the Garden of Eden. The bible also tells us that God made Adam and asked him to give names to all the animals. (Genesis 2:19 NKJV).

And what a huge task that must have been! If you do not think so, the next time you go to a zoo or to a circus and see all the animals, try to imagine what you would call them if they did not already have names. You would look at the giraffe, and I guess you would call him Mr. Longneck. Maybe you would just call him funny or tall.

So, Adam had to settle down to real business and think up very good names for all the animals. And he did it well, too. Of course, it wasn't necessary for Adam to hunt all over the garden for the various animals in order to see them and to give their names. The Bible tells us that he was made a king or a ruler over them, so they all obeyed him, and would come right up to him when he called them, just as a dog will do for us today.

Well, Adam was not only kind to all the animals, but he

was friendly with them, even with those that now are wild. He treated them just as we do the pets, we have in our homes today.

When Adam had finished naming the animals and had become familiar with them all, he made a very important discovery. He found out that there were no animals with which he could talk in the way we talk to each other. The animals were very nice, and he was glad to have them in the garden with him, but he really needed a companion who would be more like him. Wouldn't you be lonesome if there were no other girls or boys around?

The best dog in the world cannot take the place of a sibling or a friend.

Well, that is what Adam discovered. Of course, God knew this all the time because he knows everything, but he wanted Adam to find out for himself. God never meant for Adam to remain all alone in the Garden of Eden forever, but he wanted Adam to understand how much he really needed company. God knows all, so he knew that Adam would be more thankful for what he did for him.

And what did God do?

You have guessed it already! Yes, he created a real friend for Adam, who also became his wife. Her name was Eve. Pretty name, isn't it? It means "life-giver," because she was the first woman. God wanted Eve to be very much like Adam, so he made her in a very special way. He put Adam to sleep, and while he was asleep God took one of his ribs away from him, and with that rib he made Eve.

Wasn't that amazing?

In this way, you see, Eve was just like Adam—just like another part of him, yet she was separate—and they could talk together and be real friends to each other. God is certainly very wise and can do wonderful things!

There is no need for us to try to understand how God did such a wonderful thing as that. He has done many great things that we cannot understand, but they are true just the same. We cannot even understand what makes us grow, can we? Oh, you say it is because we eat good nourishing food. But that is not all there is to it. If our stomachs do not work properly, we will not grow, no matter how much we eat. Sometimes, perhaps, our stomachs get upset, and then we don't want to eat, or if we do eat, we get very sick and wish we hadn't eaten.

Suppose God had made us in such a way that we would never want to eat, or that our stomachs would always be upset. I guess we couldn't expect to grow very much then, could we? Well, that's just it. We don't understand how God made us with good stomachs, and eyes, and ears. We just know that he did, and that he made Eve, and that Adam was very glad to have Eve for a companion.

But there was one thing about Adam and Eve that was different from the rest of us. They had never been children. Can you imagine that? While we are children and growing up, we learn a lot of things, don't we? We learn that certain things are right, and that other things are wrong. We learn that if we always do what is right, we will be much happier than when we do wrong.

Well, Adam and Eve had to learn this lesson as grown-up persons, because they had never been children. God knew they needed a lesson like this, so he told them not to eat the fruit that grew on a certain tree in the garden. It was called the "tree of the knowledge of good and evil" (Genesis 2:17 NKJV). And God made it very plain to Adam and Eve that it was really wrong to eat the fruit of this tree, and if they did eat it, they would surely die.

Now there was a serpent in the garden and, being tame, it probably played where Eve could watch it.

The serpent was so cunning he made Eve believe that it would be all right to eat the fruit of that forbidden tree.

Eve told the serpent that God said you would surely die if you eat from the tree in the midst of the garden. Then the serpent said to the woman, "You will not surely die." (Genesis 3:4 NKJV).

So, Eve was persuaded to eat the fruit after all because she wanted to be just like God, knowing good and evil

Of course, the serpent wasn't really smart enough to do this all by itself. Satan caused the serpent to act that way. Satan is an enemy of God, and that is why he made the serpent deceive Eve.

Yes, Eve was deceived by that serpent and ate the forbidden fruit. And what was even worse, she coaxed Adam to eat it also. That means that Adam and Eve did what God told them not to do.

Now, the Lord had told Adam and Eve that if they disobeyed him that they "shall surely die" (Genesis 2:17, NKJV). This meant that they couldn't live forever and ever enjoying all the wonderful things in the Garden of Eden; instead, sooner or later they would become feeble and finally die.

Death is a terrible thing, isn't it? Especially when you die and do not go home to live with God.

Just think—it is because Adam and Eve did as God told them not to do (disobeyed) that people all over the world are dying! If it had not been for this, we would have lived forever in that great big Garden of Eden.

Well, Adam and Eve learned a lot in that way, didn't they? If your mother or father tells you not to put your hands on the hot stove and then you do so, you suffer for your disobedience, but you do learn that the stove is hot, so you don't put your hands on it any more. Now that is why God let Adam and Eve do what they did. He wanted them to learn for themselves that they would suffer if they did what he told them not to do.

The Bible tells us that someday God will use his great power to restore the entire world. John said, "now I saw a new heaven and a new earth, for the first heaven and the first earth had passed away." (Revelation 21:1 NKJV). In other words, God will make the earth brand new; now want that be awesome to live with God forever? When that happen Adam's garden will become bigger and bigger until it covers the whole earth.

review quiz

Who was the first man? Where did he live?

_____

_____

_____

_____

Who was the first one to give names to animals? Can you name two animals that might be a pet?

_____

_____

_____

_____

Who was the wife of the first man? Where did she come from?

_____

_____

_____

_____

Why did Adam and Eve have to leave the Garden of Eden? Will they ever return?

_____

_____

_____

_____

first two brothers

Can you imagine what it must have been like when there were only two boys in the whole wide world?

Just think what that would mean! No other children to play with—just two boys, all by themselves. Adam and Eve, the first man and the first woman, were the father and mother of these two boys. For a little while there was only one boy, and when he was born his mother named him Cain. To mother Eve, the name "Cain" meant that God had given this boy to her, and that made her very happy.

As we learned in our last story, Adam, and Eve both did

what God told them not to do. Because of this, God made them move out of the beautiful garden he had prepared for them. They didn't find things as nice outside of the garden. Fruit, vegetables, and other foods were scarce and hard to grow.

The country outside the garden was very much like a desert. The land was dry and hot, and it required a great deal of work to grow enough food to keep them from being hungry. I am sure Adam and Eve were often hungry and very tired. It was their own fault, though, because if they had obeyed God they could have stayed right in that beautiful garden where good food was plentiful, and everything was pleasant.

They must have had many wearisome and unhappy days after they had to move out of the garden, and they probably thought that God had forgotten all about them. Well, God did not forget about them even though he had to punish them, he still provided for them, isn't he a wonderful God? Now mother Eve had the right idea when Cain was born because he had been given to her by the Lord. No wonder she was happy!

It was not so very long after this that God gave Adam and Eve another boy, and his mother named him Abel. This was especially nice for Cain, for now he was no longer the only boy in the whole wide world. My, how happy Cain must have been to have a baby brother!

Do you think Cain and Abel went to school just as boys and girls do today? The Bible doesn't tell us everything they did, but I don't think they went to school as children do now.

How do I know?

Well, I don't see how there could have been schools without children, do you? As Cain and Abel were the first children, and for a long time the only children, I guess we will have to decide that they didn't go to school; at least not the kind children attend now. But don't start wishing you were Cain and Abel just because they didn't have to go to school and didn't have homework to do.

The Bible tells us that when they grew up to be young men, Cain was a vegetable farmer and Abel was a raiser of sheep. Now you can figure it out for yourself that they had to learn how to do these things while they were growing up, so in this way they went to what we might call a school, didn't they? Yes, they had much to learn.

Let's imagine that Adam, the father of these first two boys, was their schoolteacher. The reason children go to school is to learn the things they will need to know when they grow up. What Cain and Abel needed to know was how to farm and to raise sheep. Well, the very best way to learn was to help their father do those things, so I can just see Cain out in the field helping his father dig up the ground and plant the seed, and later care for the plants by pulling out the weeds.

Oh, yes, they had weeds too! The Bible calls them thorns and thistles, which are the worst kind of weeds. There weren't any weeds in the Garden of Eden, but there were plenty of them outside, and they surely did cause Adam a lot of trouble.

Adam knew that Cain also would have trouble with the weeds, so he taught him what to do with them, and how to care for the various kinds of plants he wanted to grow in order to provide food for the family. So, you see, there was a great deal for Cain to learn, and maybe his back was quite tired sometimes from tilling the soil and pulling the weeds. But that was really good for him. A little work doesn't hurt boys and girls. In fact, it makes them strong and healthy.

And it's fun, too!

When you are helping your parents with their work, just make believe it is a game, and you will really enjoy it. But if you say to yourself, "My, this is awful the way I have to work," then you won't enjoy it a bit, and it won't do you nearly as much good.

Abel had a lot of things to learn, also. He decided that when he grew to be a man, he would own a big sheep ranch. Well, there's a lot more to a sheep ranch than merely sitting down watching the sheep. You have to know how to take care of the sheep—where to find the best grass for them, and good water too. And you should know how to take care of them when they get hurt, or become ill, as sheep sometimes do, just like boys and girls. Aren't you glad that someone knows how to take care of you when you are sick?

Well, probably sheep feel the same way about it, and if Abel was to be a good shepherd that was one of the things he had to learn. So, you see, he went to school also, not in a big brick or a wooden schoolhouse, but out in the fields where he could watch the sheep and learn to do all the things necessary for them to be healthy and to grow.

Finally, school days for Cain and Abel were over. They were no longer boys, but young men. Don't try to think of them, though, as wearing long trousers, because men didn't wear trousers back in those days. Both children and grownups wore only a simple robe or cloth around their body. But I doubt if folks thought much about clothes then, as they were kept busy growing food. They couldn't go to a grocery store or a vegetable stand and buy what they wanted, because there were no such places. If they didn't grow food for themselves, they just didn't have any.

Cain and Abel must have learned their lessons well while they were growing up, because they seemed to be very successful in farming and in raising sheep. Probably both of them were hard workers, and that is very important. But even if they did work hard, Cain and Abel were very thankful to God for everything they had. Because they wanted to show God how much they appreciated what he had done for them they brought gifts to him from what he had given to them.

Gifts to God are sometimes called "offerings," and sometimes they are called "sacrifices." In those days, offerings to God were placed on an altar, which was usually a pile of stones. When God was pleased with the gift he caused it to catch on fire. Well, Cain's gift to God was from the fruits and vegetables he had grown, and Abel gave God one of his sheep. God was very much pleased with Abel's gift, but he did not accept the offering made by Cain. Of course, this was rather strange, but God had a very good reason for it. God has a good reason for everything he does. He doesn't always tell us the reason, and it is not necessary that we should know. But God always knows what is best. That is what the Bible tells us, and we know that the Bible is true!

God wants us all to learn that we should do things the way he wants them done, because he is so much wiser than we are and his way is always the best way. It's just the same as when Mother or Father wants us to do something. It might not seem right to us, but they know best.

Mother may ask Clarissa to wash the breakfast dishes, but she thinks she would rather make the beds.

Well, of course, it's a good thing to have the beds made because there's nothing wrong with that at all, but mother has a reason for wanting the dishes washed first. She may not tell Clarissa the reason, but if Clarissa is a good and obedient girl she will do what her mother wants done, whether she knows why or not.

That is the way Cain should have thought about it. When he found that God was pleased with the offering of a sheep, he could have asked Abel for a sheep. Then he could have made an offering that would have been pleasing to God. But he didn't do that. Instead, he became jealous of Abel.

Wasn't that terrible?

Just think for a moment, these two boys lived in the same house, they were raised by the same parents, and they played and worked together. Now Cain became jealous of his brother. He started to argue with Abel one day, and became so angry, well, I hate to say it, but he killed Abel.

I told you before about Satan, who also became jealous. Jealousy is an awful thing. Jealousy has a different concept than envy; let's explore these two words. Jealousy and envy concern the possession of something, for example an object or relationship with a person, both can be selfish. You see, jealousy concerns the loss of what one has, and envy concerns one not having what one wants. Never, never allow yourself to be jealous or envious. If you do, you will be very unhappy, and you may do things for which you will be very, very sorry.

The Lord was angry with Cain, so Cain was sent away. God punished him and said, "when you till the ground, it shall no longer yield its strength to you" (Genesis 4:12 NKJV) and at the same time God blessed him, "and the Lord set a mark on Cain, lest anyone finding him should kill him" (Genesis 4:15 NKJV). Isn't God awesome? You know, if we do wrong, people will surely find out about it. The only way to be happy is to do the best we can to please God.

Adam and Eve, Abel's father and mother, must have missed him terribly. But God is very good, and he gave them another son. Eve appreciated this very much. You see, when Adam and Eve did as God told them not to do, God had to send someone who would punish Satan.

God spoke of the one he would send to punish Satan as the "seed," which simply means a son, and when Eve's third son was born she said, "God has given me another 'seed.'" She named him Seth.

Yes, Eve still loved God, and was very glad to think that he would do something for her family. Of course, Seth was not the seed whom God had promised. It was to be a great many years before God would send that seed. But God has never forgotten that promise. In fact, he has already sent the real seed, or Son of promise, as we will learn in a later story. I mention it now because it shows why God was pleased with the gift Abel brought to him. The blood of Abel's lamb was shed, and this offering was like a much more wonderful offering which would be brought to God thousands of years later; one that would be very pleasing to God, brought to him by his Son, Jesus.

Jesus was God's Lamb, who shed his innocent blood so that Adam and Eve and all the people in the world can by-and-by return to the Garden of Eden, which will then be the whole earth made brand new.

review quiz

What were the names of the first two boys who ever lived?
Who were their parents?

_____

_____

_____

_____

Did the first two brothers ever go to school?

_____

_____

_____

_____

Why was God pleased with the offering that Abel made to him?

_____

_____

_____

_____

Why wasn't God pleased with the offering Cain made for him?

_____

_____

_____

_____

What type or kind of school did the first two brothers attend?

_____

_____

_____

_____

Why did Cain kill his only brother Abel?

_____

_____

_____

_____

the baby in a boat

Do you remember the story in the Bible of Noah and the big boat on the dry land?

Noah built that big boat because God asked him to build it. God knew that Noah would need such a boat, for the time was coming when it would rain and rain and rain until all the land would be covered with water and all the people and animals would be drowned, except those in Noah's boat. That was really a big boat. It was large enough for Noah, his family, and many, many animals, some of every kind. It was called an "ark."

Well, this story is not about Noah's ark, but another ark.

Not another large ark, but a very small one—just big enough to hold one little baby boy. But this little ark was used for the same reason that the big ark was used. The big ark saved Noah and all his family from being drowned, while this little ark saved one dear, little baby boy from being drowned.

And who do you suppose that baby was?

Really, the baby didn't have any name while he was in the ark. After he was taken out of the ark a very kind Egyptian princess named him Moses. The name Moses means, "to draw out," because this Egyptian princess had drawn out, or taken, the baby from the water.

But Moses was not an Egyptian boy. Oh, no! He was a little Jewish baby. They were called "Hebrews" then, which is still one of the names of the Jewish people.

The Hebrews were the children of Jacob, and all the children that have since been born from Jacob's children are called Jacob's descendants. Jacob was the grandson of Abraham.

To Abraham and his children God promised to give the land of Canaan, but at the time of this story all the Hebrew people were in Egypt. Joseph, one of Jacob's sons, had become a ruler in Egypt, and the rest of the family went there during the years of famine.

Everything went along fine with the Hebrew children as long as Joseph lived. But, like everybody else, Joseph grew old and died, and so did all his brothers. But, of course, there were a great many Hebrew children who became men and women, and they had children of their own. As years went by, there were thousands and thousands of Hebrews living in the land of Egypt.

The Egyptians grew old and died also. Everybody had to die then, just as everybody dies now, because in the Garden of Eden Adam and Eve disobeyed God.

It won't always be that way, though, for God loves everybody, and he gave his Son, Jesus, to die for everybody; and by and by Jesus will bring back all the dead people and give them health and strength, and they will then live forever. Won't that be wonderful? That's what the Bible means when it says that Jesus saves the people. He saves them from death just as the big boat saved Noah and his family from the water, and just as the little boat saved the little baby known as Moses from the water.

Well, to get back to my story, that nice, kind Pharaoh—or king—of Egypt, who had made Joseph such an important ruler over the people, died. Then there was a Pharaoh in Egypt who had not known Joseph, and he was unfriendly to Joseph's relatives.

This king saw how the Hebrew children were increasing in number, and he was afraid that someday there would be more Hebrews than Egyptians. So, what do you suppose he did? Why, he made slaves of all the Hebrews and put cruel masters over them to make them work very, very hard. Perhaps he thought this would cause them to die young and that soon there wouldn't be nearly as many Hebrews.

But God was with the Hebrews.

He had made wonderful promises to Abraham,

Isaac, Jacob, and to all of Jacob's sons. These promises belonged to all the Hebrews. They were God's people, and God won't let anybody kill all of his people.

Besides, God will bring back to life all the Hebrews who have died, and everybody else, too, for that matter. You see, God always keeps his promises, and no one can really interfere with what God wants done.

That's a very important thing to remember.

Making slaves of the Hebrews didn't stop them from increasing in number, so the king of Egypt ordered that all the boy babies of the Hebrews should be killed as soon as they were born. They were to be thrown into the river Nile and drowned. Wasn't that awful?

Now the mother of the baby boy who was later named Moses dearly loved that little child, just as all of us love babies today, and no matter what the king had said, she made up her mind that she would do all she could to keep him from being drowned.

She kept the baby out of sight in her home for three months, and when she realized that she couldn't keep him hidden much longer, she built that little boat of bulrushes and painted it with tar so it wouldn't leak. Then she placed the baby in the ark and hid it among the leaves and grass that grew up at the edge of the water in the river.

After the mother put this small boat with its precious passenger by the edge of the river, she went away. But the baby's sister stood nearby to see what would happen. And what do you think did occur? Why, one of the daughters of the king—the very king who had ordered all the Hebrew baby boys killed— came down to the river to bathe. Several young ladies came with her to give her any help she needed.

The king's daughter saw the little boat snuggled among the reeds and bulrushes by the water's edge, and she asked her servants to find out what was in it.

When they opened the basket, there was that darling baby! Of course, the king's daughter knew that it was a Hebrew baby. She knew, too, that all Hebrew boy babies were supposed to be drowned. But she was tenderhearted and couldn't bear to see such a precious little baby killed, so she decided that she would adopt the baby and call it her own. Wasn't that wonderful?

You see, God had planned that when this particular boy became a man, he would give him a great work to do, and this was God's way of saving the boy he wanted to use. God always knows how to do what he wants to do.

That's why we should always trust him and believe that his promises will come true.

Are you feeling more secure as to how important you are to God?

The king's daughter knew that she didn't understand very much about taking care of babies, so just at the right time the baby's own sister, who had stayed nearby to see what would happen, came to her and offered to get a nurse to take care of the baby. The king's daughter thought this was a very good idea, so the baby's sister went home and brought back their mother.

When she came, Pharaoh's daughter asked her to take the baby and nurse him for her. Now, didn't everything turn out well? That is the way the Lord does things. Then the king's daughter named the baby Moses, and his own mother cared for Moses until he grew to be a young man.

review quiz

Explain how it come about that Moses was cared for and educated in the home of Egypt's ruler?

_____

_____

_____

_____

Did the King's daughter know how to care for a baby?

_____

_____

_____

_____

Why was Moses put in a small ark at the edge of a river when he was a baby?

_____

_____

_____

_____

Who nursed Moses when he was a baby?

_____

_____

_____

_____

let the children come to me

Who is Pharaoh?

_____

_____

_____

_____

god speaks and moses listens

Perhaps you are wondering how the little boy Moses got along after the king's daughter found him in that tiny, basket-like boat floating around among the leaves at the edge of the river. He was well taken care of, you may be sure, because, as I told you, the king's daughter hired Moses' own mother to nurse him.

Really, you see it was God who was taking care of Moses, because God had a great work for him to do and nothing whatsoever can harm those whom God wishes to protect. Just because that wicked Pharaoh, the king of Egypt, decided that all baby boys of the Hebrews should be killed, it didn't mean that God couldn't take care of Moses, just as He takes care of you. That's why children have a special place in God's heart.

That is something we should always remember.

And now you are probably wondering what great work God had for Moses to do.

Well, as you know, Egypt was not the country God promised to the Hebrew people, the children of Abraham. They were in Egypt because years and years before this, Joseph, one of the twelve sons of Jacob, was sold by his brothers as a slave and taken there, and later he became a great ruler over the people.

Then, when there was a famine in Canaan, the real home of the Hebrews, the rest of the family also went to Egypt, where they were cared for by Joseph. I am sure you remember that wonderful story. It's a true story, too, because it is in the Bible, and we know that the Bible is true.

But now the Hebrew people were having a very hard time in Egypt. They were all slaves, and God wanted to deliver them from their taskmasters and take them back into the land of Canaan that he had promised to their father, Abraham. God knew that when Moses became a man he would be just the right person to lead all the Israelites out of Egypt, so that is why God was taking care of him.

And God knew something else, too! God knows everything. He knows things even before they happen!

God knew that Pharaoh, the king of Egypt, would not want to let the Israelites leave the country. You see, they were doing a lot of hard work for the Egyptians, and if they left, the Egyptians would have to do this work themselves. So, you can be sure that Pharaoh did all he could to keep them in Egypt.

God knew that whoever was to lead his people out of Egypt would need to know how to talk to the king, for he would have to appear before him to ask permission for the Hebrews to leave. Wasn't it wonderful how God arranged for Moses to learn all he needed to know so that he could do this? You see, he was being cared for and educated right in the royal palace.

But there was someone who spent more time with Moses than anyone else in the palace, and that was his own mother. Moses' dear mother knew about God's promise to Abraham, and she knew that the Hebrews were merely visitors in Egypt. You may be sure that she would keep telling Moses about the many wonderful things God had done for their people, and what he had promised to do for them. She would tell him about Abraham, Isaac, Jacob, and the promise God had made to them of a time coming when he would bless all the people of the world, and that the one to do this would come from the Hebrew people.

The Jewish people believed these wonderful promises of God. They believed God would raise up a man from among them to be this great leader, and that through him all of God's promises would come true.

The Hebrew name for this great leader was "Messiah."

But the other nations didn't believe God's promises, and they thought the Jewish people were foolish to believe in a coming Messiah. It is the same today. A great many people think we are foolish to believe the promises of the Bible, but such people are very much mistaken. Don't ever think it is foolish to believe that the promises of the Bible will come true.

Moses' mother believed the promises of God, and so did Moses. And Moses didn't care if the Egyptians did think he was foolish. He believed God's promises just the same. You can see that Moses must have had a hard time while he was growing up. He believed what his mother told him about God and the promises of God, and the Egyptians in the king's palace probably made fun of him. Maybe they told him he was crazy; but he did not care what the Egyptians thought of him, because he knew better.

review quiz

Was Egypt the country God promised to the Hebrew people? If not, what was the name of the country?

_____

_____

_____

_____

Why was Moses so important to God? Why did He spend time preparing Moses for his mission?

_____

_____

_____

_____

What is the Hebrew name for our great leader?

_____

_____

_____

_____

Who didn't believe God's promises?

_____

_____

_____

_____

a wise man
and a king

Now I want to tell you about a wise man who ruled over the children of Israel and a king who was made very wise by God.

After he became king he had a dream. In this dream God asked him to make a request for something which he would very much like to have. What would you ask for if you had such an opportunity?

I haven't told you the name of this king who was made so

wise, have I? Well, his name was Solomon. He was the son of David, the shepherd boy who became king of Israel. David ruled over Israel for forty years, and during all that time he had plenty of trouble. Enemies were fighting against Israel during nearly all his reign, so David had a very stormy time. But Solomon didn't have nearly the amount of trouble during the time he was king.

When David grew very old and knew that he would not live much longer, he gave orders that his son Solomon should be the king. David wasn't a bit jealous; you see. He knew he was too old to be king any longer, and he wanted the Israelites to have a king who could look after them. So, he said that Solomon was to be their ruler. That was an easy way for Solomon to become king, wasn't it? All the time that Solomon was king the enemies of Israel didn't fight against them. Thus, Solomon was a king of peace, while David had been a king of war.

Solomon could have decided that plenty of money would be the best thing for him, or that he needed a very large army to protect the Israelites against their enemies. He may have thought of these things, but he decided that what he needed most of all was wisdom, so he asked God to make him wise. He wanted to be wise in order to rule over God's people in the right way. God was pleased with this request, so he made this king the wisest of all the kings who ever ruled over the Israelites.

God was so pleased that Solomon had asked for wisdom instead of asking for gold to make him rich that he gave the king both wisdom and riches. Of course, God does not make everyone as wise as Solomon, even if they ask him to do so. That was a very special favor to Solomon, to help him rule wisely over the children of Israel. It was David's dying wish that God would give his son Solomon his blessing—that he would be upright and just in all his dealings. And when Solomon showed that his first thought was to honor God by offering sacrifices to him, God told him he would grant his request for that which he desired.

Yes, God made Solomon rich as well as wise. God also helped him to build a temple. The temple was to take the place of the tabernacle. Now, the tabernacle was God's house! The tabernacle was God's house because it was there that he gave his blessings to the priests, that the priests might give them to the people. The tabernacle was built in a very special way so that it could be taken apart and moved from place to place. When it was built the Israelites were wandering around in the desert, and every time they moved, God's house was moved with them. So it had to be made easy to move.

But now the Israelites were no longer wandering in the wilderness. They were in the Promised Land, and had been there for a long time, but they were still using the tabernacle. King David decided that the Lord should have a more permanent house than that movable tabernacle, and God was very much pleased that David felt this way about it. But God didn't let David build the new house for him. David prepared some of the lumber and stones for it, but God told him that the building of the new house would have to wait until his son Solomon was king.

Now it was this new house that was called the temple. It was built to be very sturdy and put together so firmly that it wouldn't be possible to move it from place to place in the way the tabernacle had been moved. But it was God's house, and it was used in the same way as the tabernacle. The tabernacle was like a tent, but the temple was like a house.

When you go out hiking or fishing for a few days you sometimes live in a tent, and you take the tent right along with you. In that way you have a place to sleep every night. That is very good. But when you arrive home you don't sleep in the tent any more. Then you have a real house in which to live.

Well, it was something like that with the house of God. The tabernacle was fine while they were moving so often, but now they were in their own land, and one day Solomon built a real house for God. And my, what a wonderful house—or temple—it was! When you read about it in the Bible, you will wonder where Solomon found all the gold that he used in building it.

First, there were the ceiling beams, and the floor joists, all of which were covered over with cedar boards. Then these cedar boards were covered with gold, and the floorboards were covered with gold. It was really a very beautiful house. You can imagine how wonderful it was when I tell you that it took more than seven years to build.

This was God's house, and Solomon loved God and wanted him to have the very best of everything. That's the way we should all feel about God. Let us remember this, so that whatever we do for God we will do the very best we possibly can.

When the temple was completed and the priests first entered it to serve the Lord as they had done in the tabernacle, suddenly it was filled with smoke. I suppose you think it caught on fire, but that was not so. No, God caused that smoke to fill the temple. It was God's way of saying to the priests and to Solomon and to all the Israelites, that he was pleased with what had been done for him. The Bible tells us that this smoke was the glory of God. When God shows his glory we know he is pleased.

Then King Solomon offered a very long prayer to God, and in this prayer, he said many very wonderful things. One thing he said was that God did not really need this new house at all. He said that all the heavens which are above us are not large

let the children come to me

enough for God to use as a house, and that we could not expect God to live in a house we might build for him, even though we did use millions and millions and millions of dollars' worth of gold to build it.

Solomon was right!

God didn't need that temple at all, but the Israelites needed it. They needed God's blessings. The tabernacle and the temple were the places where God give his blessings to the people. God had asked Moses to build the tabernacle, and now he was pleased with the temple, because it showed how by-and-by he will give his blessings to the whole world through a temple made of people instead of stones, boards, and gold.

Just remember this, the temple Solomon built for God was just like a beautiful picture of a more wonderful temple, a temple from which good things will go out to everyone all over the whole wide world.

Solomon was certainly very wise and very rich. The whole nation of Israel became prosperous during the time he was king. He had merchant vessels, and these brought gold from Ophir, and they also brought spices and horses and mules, and even monkeys and peacocks from distant places.

A very famous queen of another country, known as the Queen of Sheba, heard of the great wisdom and riches of Solomon, but thought it couldn't possibly be true. So, she decided to visit Solomon to find out for herself. You know, that's the way some people are about the Bible. They just can't believe that all the wonderful things in it are really true. But we know that whatever the Bible says is true!

The Bible tells us about a king who is much more wonderful than Solomon. He is King Jesus. King Jesus is wiser than Solomon, richer than Solomon, more powerful than Solomon.

And just like Solomon, but in a much better way, King Jesus will be a King of peace.

It's interesting to read about King Solomon, but how much better it will be to enjoy all the good things that King Jesus will do for the people! The Bible tells us this, and we know that the Bible is true.

review quiz

Who was the king of Israel after David died, and why was he so wise?

_____

_____

_____

_____

What was Solomon's Temple, and why is it called the house of the Lord?

_____

_____

_____

_____

Why did Solomon ask God for wisdom instead of riches?

_____

_____

_____

_____

Do you know of a King who is wiser and richer than King Solomon?

_____

_____

_____

_____

let the children come to me

manger baby

Some people think that when George Washington was born he was the world's most important baby, but anyone who thinks that would be wrong, because when Jesus was born he was the most important baby. No baby ever born before Jesus was nearly so important, and no baby born since has been as important as Jesus. When Jesus was born it meant that many, many of the wonderful promises of God had come true, and that all the rest of his promises were sure to come true later.

That is what made him important.

Jesus was born in a manger where cattle are fed. I'll tell you why that was so. His mother and foster father lived in a town called Nazareth. The people of Israel no longer had a king of their own but were being ruled by the Romans. The Roman government was getting ready to tax all the people, so Jesus' parents had to go to Bethlehem to sign their names on the Roman tax books.

A great many other people were visiting in Bethlehem at that time, and when Jesus' parents arrived, there just wasn't any room for them. All the hotels were filled, and a barn was the only place they could find in which to stay overnight.

And that is where baby Jesus was born!

But that didn't really make any difference. It is not where people are born that really counts isn't it? And the most important thing of all is what God thinks about us. Jesus was God's own Son, and God loved him and had a wonderful work for him to do.

A very wonderful thing occurred on the night Jesus was born.

Imagine a group of shepherds out in the fields near Bethlehem, caring for their sheep. Suddenly they heard the most beautiful music, and it seemed to be in the sky above them. They looked up and saw that the sky was very bright. No doubt they were frightened because this was unusual. Then they heard an angel telling them not to be afraid. The angel told the shepherds that he had good news for them then joyfully told them that Christ was born that night and that he would save the people of Israel from their sins. Wasn't that wonderful?

"Christ" is another name for Jesus. It means that Jesus is the one whom God chose to save his people. For hundreds and hundreds of years God had been promising to send Christ and now the angel told the shepherds he would be born as a little baby that night, and that they would find him in a manger in

Bethlehem. My, those shepherds must have been excited, and glad, too!

After the angel told the shepherds this good news, a great many angels began to sing, and their song told the shepherds that there was to be peace on earth, and that God had sent his Son because of his good will toward all the people of the earth. Yes, God loved all the people, and now he was getting ready to make his many promises to bless them come true. What a wonderful night that was!

The shepherds went to Bethlehem and there found the baby, the wonderful baby, whom God had sent. They worshipped the child and gave thanks to God because he was making his promises come true. God's promise was that Jesus would be a great king to rule over the whole earth. This is the King Jesus we will discuss later.

In a faraway country east of Palestine there were wise men. Well, they learned that Jesus was born, and that he was to be a great king, so they decided they also would travel to Bethlehem to visit the newborn king.

But when these wise men arrived in the land of the Israelites, they decided that first they would visit King Herod, who was then the king. He was a ruler appointed by the supreme ruler of the whole Roman world. This supreme ruler was called the "Caesar," after Julius Caesar, and Herod was a king under the Caesar.

For the most part, Caesar gave Herod the power to do whatever he wanted to do. Well, the wise men visited Herod, and told him that Jesus, a little Jewish boy, had been born and that he would grow up to be a great king. Herod didn't like this at all, and he decided he would have that baby killed.

But Herod did not tell the wise men what he planned to do. No, he deceived them. He told them to go and find the child and come back to him and let him know where Jesus lived, as he also wanted to go and worship the new king. Herod was a clever liar, but God was taking care of Jesus. The wise men found the young child and the mother, who were now living in a house in Bethlehem, and they gave him the presents they had brought and worshipped him just as they had planned.

One day you will learn to know when God is talking to you and hopefully you will obey, just like the wise men.

The day had ended, so they remained overnight before starting back. That night they dreamed that it would be wrong to visit Herod on the way back to tell him where he could find Jesus, as he had asked them to do. You see, God gave them this dream, and from it they learned that they were to return to the East by another road so Herod wouldn't find out anything at all about Jesus. The wise men obeyed what God told them in the dream, so Herod's plan to find the child and destroy him failed.

When Herod learned that the wise men had returned to the East by another way, he was very angry. He didn't know where to find Jesus. All he knew was that a future king had been born, and he wanted to kill this baby before he grew up to be a king. Herod did a dreadful thing.

He gave orders that all the little baby boys of the Jews in Bethlehem and in the surrounding country should be killed. He thought that if all these babies were killed the baby Jesus would certainly be among them and would be killed also.

Wasn't that terrible?

Of course, all those babies will be brought back to life again. The Bible tells us that they shall come back from "the land of the enemy." The land of the enemy is the land of death; so, we know that they are coming back from death. God told the Prophet Jeremiah to write down that promise. It is found in the book of Jeremiah, chapter 31, verses 16 and 17.

But Jesus wasn't killed when all the other Jewish babies were killed, because God was taking care of him. If God had allowed anything to happen to the baby Jesus, then all of his wonderful promises could not have come true.

So what did God do?

Well, that same night he caused Joseph, the foster father of Jesus, to have a dream also. Joseph dreamed that it was necessary for him and his wife, Mary, the mother of Jesus, to flee into Egypt and take Jesus with them. So they went to Egypt right away. Thus Jesus escaped being killed.

The Bible doesn't tell us any more about Jesus until he was twelve years old. By that time Herod, who tried to kill Jesus, was dead, so it was safe for Joseph and his family to return to their home in Nazareth. After they had returned to Nazareth, they visited the temple in Jerusalem and there Jesus talked with the teachers in the temple.

He was so interested that he didn't know his parents had started home without him. They thought he was with others in the company returning home with them. But when they could not find him among any of their friends and relatives, they returned to Jerusalem where they found him in the temple. His mother reproved him for causing them so much trouble and anxiety. He asked them if they didn't know it was necessary for him to be doing what his Father wanted him to do.

I don't know whether or not they understood what he meant but, you see, God was the Father of Jesus, and Jesus knew even as a twelve-year-old that his Father had a great work for him to do.

When God gave his Law to Moses, and Moses gave it to the people of Israel, there was one part of it which said that anyone "from thirty years old and above, even to fifty years old, all who enter the service to do the work in the tabernacle of meeting" (Numbers 4:3 NKJV). The bible tells us that Jesus was only twelve years old when he was in the temple asking questions, and he learned that he would have to wait until he was about thirty years old before he could start doing the work that his Father wanted him to do (Luke 3:23 NKJV).

Jesus' foster father was a carpenter, so he went back home with him and worked as a carpenter for eighteen years. I think he must have been a wonderful carpenter, don't you?

review quiz

Who was the world's most important baby, and what did it mean when he was born?

_____

_____

_____

_____

Where was Jesus born, and to whom did God announce his birth?

_____

_____

_____

_____

Who were the wise men, and why were they warned not to return to Herod after they had seen Jesus?

_____

_____

_____

_____

How did King Herod try to kill Jesus?

_____

_____

_____

let the children come to me

jesus, king of
all kings

We talked about the wisest king of men, Solomon; now we will talk about the king of kings, Jesus. Jesus is a king that cannot do wrong.

Jesus always did what God wanted him to do! Satan, the devil, tried to make Jesus do things that God did not want him to do, but Jesus always did what was right. I hope you remember the story of Adam and Eve in the Garden of Eden. If you do, you know that Adam and Eve took the devil's advice and did what God did not want them to do. It was because of this that they lost their beautiful home in the garden and grew old and died.

Now Jesus had come into the world to help everybody get perfect life back again, and the devil tried very hard to make Jesus do wrong so he couldn't bring this great blessing to the people and thus make God's promises come true.

When Jesus was baptized in the river Jordan and the power of God came upon him, he knew that he could do many wonderful things he could not have done before. Jesus could now perform miracles. Maybe you don't know what a miracle is. Well, a miracle is doing that which boys and girls and grown-up folks cannot perform. After God's power came upon Jesus he could do many wonderful things.

We can't make a beautiful flower, can we? But God makes them.

Did I hear someone say that flowers grow? Of course they do, but who makes them grow? It is God. We can watch flowers grow, but we don't actually understand what causes them to grow, nor do we actually know why one flower is red and another pink. Well, God, who created everything, knows.

And so, boys and girls, I want you to remember that because the power of God came upon Jesus, he could do things we can't understand. It is very important to remember this, because I will be telling you of many wonderful things Jesus did, and I want you to believe that he really did them. The Bible says so, and we know that the Bible is true.

After the power of God came upon Jesus he was very happy and so interested in what God wanted him to do that he went into the wilderness to pray and to think about all God's wonderful works. He didn't eat anything for forty days. My, that was a long time to go without food, wasn't it? Then, of course, Jesus was very hungry, and the devil told him that he should use the power of God to make bread out of stones so he would have something to eat.

The Bible tells us that the devil tempted Jesus.

Do you know what it means to be tempted? It is wanting or being asked to do that which we know is wrong. Jesus knew that it was wrong for him to use the power of God to make bread out of stones in order to satisfy his hunger.

Why did Jesus know that this was wrong?

Boys and girls, I want to tell you something now that I hope you will always remember. It is this: try always to think of what you can do for other people before you think of what you would like to do for yourself. That is the way God wants us to be. That's what we call being unselfish.

Well, the power of God was upon Jesus to enable him to do wonderful things for other people. It would have been wrong for him to use that power for himself. Jesus knew that he would find food after awhile, and preferred to go hungry for a short time longer rather than to use God's power to make bread for himself out of stones.

This is a lesson that all boys and girls, and men and women too, will have to learn. If you remember this story, and try always to think of others before you think of yourselves, you will be really and truly happy. It is God's way to be happy.

God is always doing things for others.

And just think of all the wonderful things he has promised to do for us! We want to be like God, don't we? Yes, that's the way God wants us to be, for he knows that is the very best thing for us.

review quiz

Did Jesus ever do wrong?

_____

_____

_____

_____

Why would it have been wrong for Jesus to make bread out of stone?

_____

_____

_____

_____

Why is it important to remember this story?

_____

_____

_____

_____

Who do you want to be like more and more each and every day of your life?

_____

_____

_____

_____